STICK to SAFE

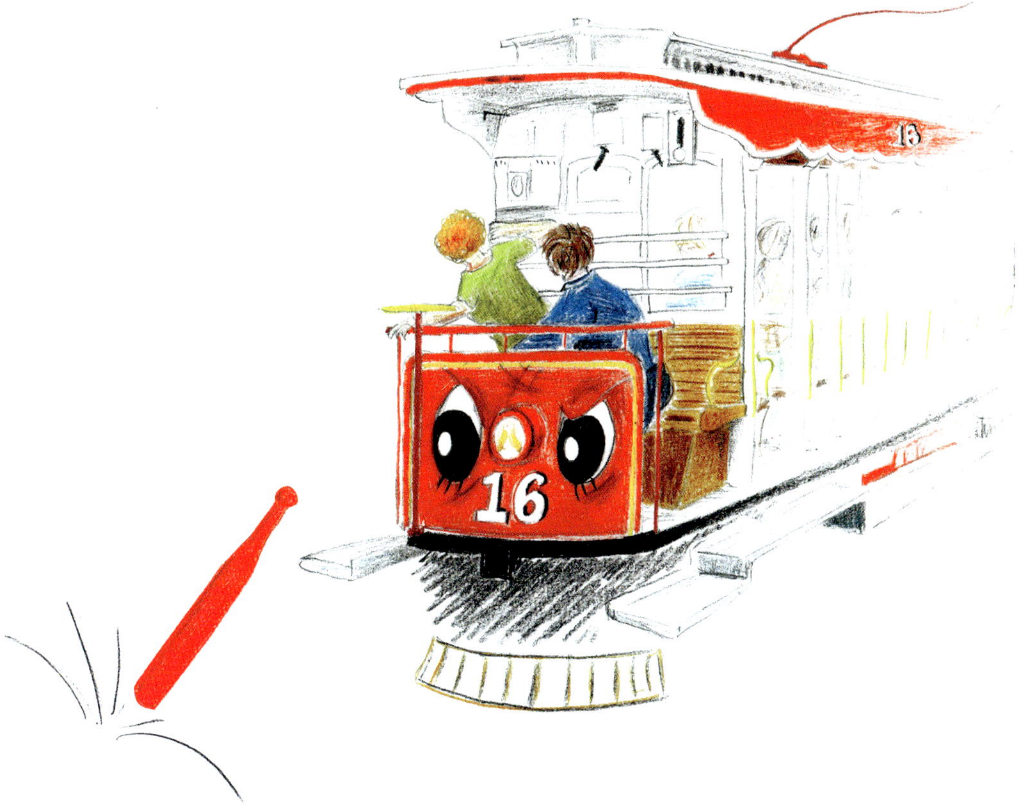

Sara Goodwins

Tram Tales of the  Manx Electric Railway

Loaghtan Books
Caardee
Dreemskerry Hill
Maughold
Isle of Man
IM7 1BE

Published by Loaghtan Books

First published: April 2018

Copyright © Sara Goodwins, 2018

All rights reserved. No part of this publication may be reproduced, stored on a retrieval system or transmitted in any form or by any means without prior permission of the publishers.

Typesetting and origination by:
Loaghtan Books

Printed and bound by:
Latimer Trend

Website: www.loaghtanbooks.com

ISBN: 978-1-908060-20-4

For
Pam's Motorman.
He knows who he is...

Tram Tales of the Manx Electric Railway

1 Something on the Line
2 Stick to Safety

CONTENTS

Chapter 1	Pam the Paddlebox (Number 16) was annoyed.	**5**
Chapter 2	The Set (which was Tramspeak for a tram and trailer) reached...	**7**
Chapter 3	The people didn't notice...	**16**
Chapter 4	Meanwhile Pam and Tina had got to Laxey.	**24**

CHAPTER 1

Pam the Paddlebox (Number 16) was annoyed. For a long time she had been the only tram painted green. She liked being different. OK, yes, Sven the Number 7 was the only tram who was blue, but his blue wasn't nearly as bright as her green.

Now she was red, just like most of the other trams. Two of the other trams had been painted green over the winter, while she'd been painted red. *They'd* got *her* colour. It wasn't even as though they looked good in it, thought Pam crossly.

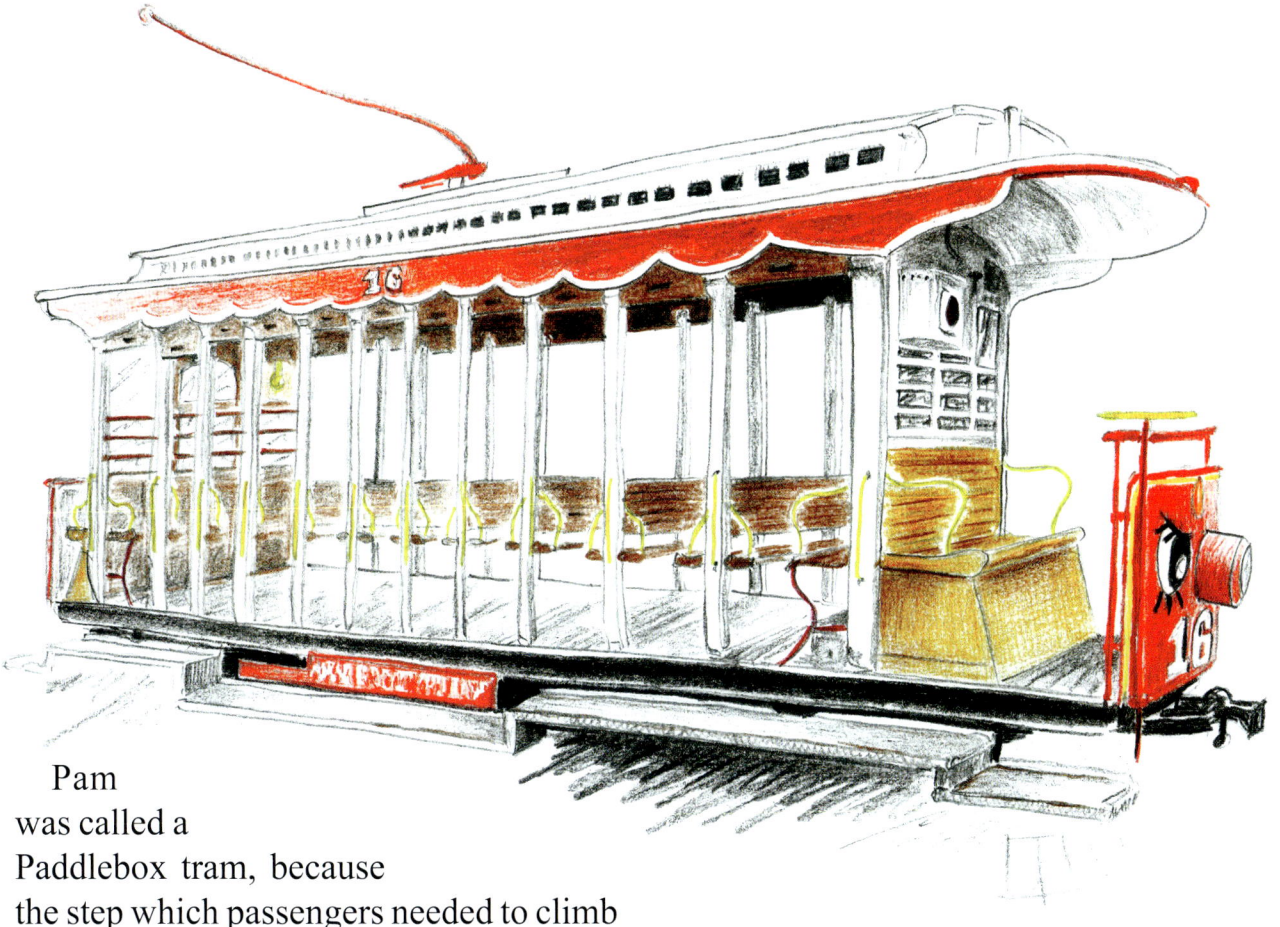

Pam was called a Paddlebox tram, because the step which passengers needed to climb aboard, wasn't completely flat. It looked a bit like the top of a castle where it went up and down to miss her wheels.

'Never mind, Pam', said her Motorman, 'you're still my favourite tram no matter what colour you are.' Everyone knew that Pam's Motorman liked her best, so she wasn't as pleased as she should have been.

As Pam hauled trailer Tina (Number 60) up the hill out of Douglas it was a lovely sunny day. All her passengers were enjoying sitting on her and Tina in the open air, but Pam was still grumbling. Even her Motorman seemed to have forgotten about her as he was talking to a passenger riding on the front seat next to him.

She began to wonder what she could do to get herself noticed again.

CHAPTER 2

The Set (which was Tramspeak for a tram and trailer) reached Ballameanagh and slowed down. Pam had been sulking and not paying attention; she had forgotten that there was Single Line Working.

Normally the trams ran along the left-hand track so that they could pass each other safely. Cars did the same on roads. If everyone stayed on their own track then there was no

danger of hitting something coming the other way.

Sometimes, however, something went wrong with the track or the wire. When that happened the trams had to share the same track, whichever way they were going, while the problem was put right.

Using the same track for both directions was called Single Line Working, and Special Rules made sure that trams didn't bump into each other. That was dangerous so the Special Rules made everything safe.

The Special Rules were very easy to understand. They were about a bright red Staff. Pam had grumpily told her Motorman that it looked like a painted stick, and was surprised when he told her that it *was* a painted stick.

'Why call it a Staff, then?' she grumbled. He only laughed and patted her controller.

The red Staff was like a rounders' bat – not that Pam had ever seen a rounders' bat – and all the trams knew that if they were carrying the Staff they were allowed to use the line where there was Single Line Working. If they didn't have the Staff, they had to stop at the beginning of that piece of line as it meant that another tram might be coming the other way.

Simple. And safe.

A red Staff. Pam was so sick of red.

Of course if the trams were using just one line then they needed to be able to get onto it. They did this by using a special piece of track which connected the two lines. As they crossed over from one track to the other, the special connecting piece of track was called a Crossover. Sometimes it meant that they had to go backwards to change from one track to the other. All the passengers thought this great fun, although the trams didn't like not being able to see where they were going.

There were several of these Crossovers up and down the line as the tramway couldn't shut too much of the track at one time or the timetable wouldn't work and passengers would be late. And cross.

Today's Single Line Working went from the Crossover at Ballameanagh to the Crossover at Fairy Cottage.

Pam's conductor had the Staff so Pam knew she was allowed to carry on.

As she trundled along the Single Line Section she watched carefully. She was still grumpy, but good trams always kept an extra special look out during Single Line Working.

At Garwick she saw why the other line was closed. The things holding the wire up had got damaged and Thrust the Thirty Three, one of the newest and strongest trams, had towed Wesley the Wire Car to where the wire needed mending. Wesley and his team of people looked after the wires which ran above the rails and which the trams needed to go along. People called it the Overhead, but Wesley always called it the Overpole.

He and his people were mending it.

The team waved to Pam and Tina as they went slowly past and Pam whistled to tell them that she'd seen them. Wesley, being a trailer, didn't have a whistle, but smiled at Pam and Tina. He would have rattled his tower at them, but one of his people was standing on it. Wesley was concentrating very hard to make sure that the wire was put back in exactly the right place for the tram poles to touch it smoothly.

Wesley didn't like the Overpole being broken, but loved being out of the shed. It got very boring being in there all the time.

Wesley lived in the Laxey shed and Pam didn't have a sleepover at Laxey very often, so she didn't know him very well. She smiled rather nervously at him.

Soon Pam got to Fairy Cottage and saw Twain (Number 22) waiting for her. He had to wait as he didn't have the Staff, so wasn't allowed into the Single Line Section.

Twain's passengers were leaning off Tommy Trailer, taking photographs. His conductor was standing on the track and watching them closely to make sure they stayed out of Pam's way.

Pam preened at all the attention, but then remembered that she was no longer green. Her red paint must make her look like everyone else she thought. Boring! She wanted to stand out.

Pam's conductor was holding the red Staff and got up from his seat on her back platform. As Pam rolled slowly past Twain, his conductor took the red Staff from her conductor. Twain whistled his thanks.

Pam headed off to Laxey, and Twain and Tommy carefully crossed over from one track to the other. They had the Staff so it was safe to go onto the Single Line Section. The line they were using was usually used by trams going the other way.

'I like running on the Wrong Line,' said Twain to his motorman. 'I've been up and down the line hundreds of times, but on the Wrong Line it all looks a bit different.'

'You make sure you concentrate properly, Twain,' said his motorman. 'It not only looks different, all the corners and everything will feel different too. We don't want to make any mistakes.'

Twain concentrated. He was one of the youngest in the fleet and wanted to be a Very Good Tram.

When it was busy, the trams often went from Douglas to Ramsey and back three times in one day. That meant that they did over 100 miles a day so got quite tired.

On her third trip up from Douglas, Pam was feeling even more grumpy. 'They're working me too hard,' she thought. 'I'm overloaded with all these passengers. If they had to work as hard as me…' She thought about losing her lovely green paint and felt even crosser.

It was a lovely day and Pam and Tina were very full. She had so many passengers on board that they were even sitting with her motorman and conductor.

That was probably why it happened.

The Set was in the Single Line Section so, of course, Pam had the Staff. It was tucked behind the conductor's bag on her back platform. Pam and Tina swept across the road near Ballabeg, and their passengers all waved at the cars waiting. One man on the back platform leaned over to look back, and was grabbed by the conductor. Leaning Out was Very Dangerous and Not Allowed because of the poles on either side. The conductor told the man to sit down again and the other people on the seat moved up to make room. While they were all shuffling along, someone's foot moved the conductor's bag. The red Staff slipped from behind it and fell off the tram.

Pam and Tina were just before the waiting hut at Ballabeg and the Staff fell onto the cess, which is Tramspeak for the edge of the trackway. Then it rolled down the bank and splashed into the stream. They were in the Single Line Section Without the Staff.

CHAPTER 3

The people didn't notice that the Staff had gone, but Trailer Tina did. She was coupled up (which meant attached) to Pam just behind the back platform. Tina couldn't see much because Pam was so close, but she couldn't help noticing a bright red stick whizz past her wheels.

'Pam! *Pam!*' she called.

'What?' whistled Pam angrily. She had just pulled Tina and all the passengers up the hill from Garwick and was tired and hot.

'PAM!
The Staff fell off you!'

Tina was very worried. She might be a trailer but she knew the rules as well as any of the trams. In fact she was older than many of the trams and so sometimes knew more than they did.

Pam was also shocked and a bit frightened. No Staff!

Then she thought 'serve them right'. Being Red was Rubbish, she'd always said so. If the Staff had been green – a much better colour – she was sure it wouldn't have happened.

'Don't tell anyone,' she told Tina.

'But…', said Tina.

'I told you not to tell anyone,' said Pam, 'the conductor should have noticed. If he didn't it's his fault. It's nothing to do with us.'

Tina said nothing. She liked their conductor, and even when they had a conductor she didn't like, the tram, trailer and crew were a team. They should stick up for each other. But she was a Trailer and had to do as she was told
by her Tram.

She wasn't happy At All.

Soon Pam got to Fairy Cottage again, and again saw Twain waiting for her. His conductor was waiting with his motorman for the Staff.

Pam rolled slowly past, laughing to herself. Her conductor was rummaging around on the back platform and eventually rang the bell three times to tell the motorman they needed to stop At Once.

Pam stopped and her motorman jumped down and walked back to find out what was wrong. Tina heard the conductor whisper that he couldn't find the Staff. The motorman looked horrified and started to help the conductor look.

Then Twain's conductor crunched along the line to find out what the problem was.

Tina looked miserable.

Pam's conductor was upset:

'I had it, I'm sure I did. We're not allowed into the Single Line Section without it – you know that.'

Pam's motorman was looking worried too. It was up to him to make sure that the Staff was on the tram. It might ride with the conductor, but he wasn't allowed to drive onto the Single Line Section without seeing it. The Staff had been given to his conductor, he was sure it had. Really quite sure. Of course.

By this time Twain's motorman had climbed down and joined the other motorman and two conductors and they all started to hunt for the Staff. Even the passengers were searching, but nobody could find it.

The Staff had gone.

Twain, waiting patiently with Tommy Trailer (who'd dozed off), didn't know what was wrong. Pam had gone past him, but he could talk to Tina:

'What's up, Tina? What are they looking for?' Very quietly Tina said:

'The Staff. They can't find it.' She was ashamed. She couldn't say that she knew where it had gone, not without Pam's permission. Yet it was all wrong that they were holding everyone up like this.

'The STAFF!' said Twain. 'But you shouldn't be in the Single Line Section without the **STAFF**.' He was horrified.

'I know,' muttered Tina.

From in front, Pam stopped pretending that she didn't know there was anything wrong:

'It's not our fault if they've forgotten it,' she said snappily.

The two motormen and two conductors were trying to decide what to do. Pam's conductor rang the stationmaster at Laxey to ask. He knew he'd get into trouble, but without the Staff Twain couldn't use the Single Line Section, and what would happen to his passengers? They were already very late.

The stationmaster was angry. Going through the Single Line Section without the Staff wasn't safe. They couldn't be sure that one of the other trams didn't have the Staff and might be coming the other way. At the same time, they couldn't leave the passengers stranded where they were.

He told Pam to carry on to Laxey, and told Twain to wait where he was. Then he rang both the other stations, and all the trams who were working up and down the line, and asked if anyone else had the Staff. It took a long time for everyone to check. They all looked very carefully.

No-one had seen it.

Then the stationmaster had to find out exactly where everyone was. Even if it made everyone very late, there mustn't be an accident. Safety came first.

Once he'd found out where they were, he told all the other trams not to go into the Single Line Section for Any Reason. It was Absolutely NOT Allowed, no matter how late they were. If they got to where the Single Line Section started they had to stop and ring him Straight Away.

Once the stationmaster had done all this he rang Twain's conductor and motorman:

'I know you don't have the Staff but I'm giving you permission to go into the Single Line Section. Only by doing that can you take your passengers home. You must be very, very careful. Don't go too fast and make sure you watch out for trouble. I don't think there is anything coming the other way, but without the Staff we can't be completely sure.'

Twain was very solemn. He might be the youngest tram but he felt very grown up as he crossed over to start along the Single Line Section. His conductor looked worried and even Tommy Trailer was keeping a careful watch. Twain's motorman was very tense:

'Careful now, Twain, don't go fast and watch carefully. Tell me at once if you see anything coming this way.' Twain knew all that of course, but he also knew his motorman was worried, so didn't mind being told.

'Shall I whistle at corners?' he asked.

'That's a very good idea, Twain,' said his motorman approvingly. 'Yes, we'll do that.'

So, at every corner, as well as every crossing, Twain whistled to show that he was coming.

Would he meet anything? He didn't know.

CHAPTER 4

Meanwhile Pam and Tina had got to Laxey. All her passengers had got off, some of them grumbling at how slow the journey had been, and quite a lot of them saying how Pam had made them late for tea. Pam was upset. She hadn't meant things to go wrong like this. She just wanted to let everyone know how much she wanted to be green again. Tina wasn't speaking to her, and her nice motorman and conductor were in the stationmaster's office. She could hear him shouting.

Eventually she swallowed her pride and asked Tina quietly:
  'Are you sure the Staff fell off me?'
  'Yes,' said Tina firmly.
  'Do you know where it is?'
  '*Yes!*' said Tina, even more firmly. Pam sighed.

At the same time, in the office, Pam's motorman was very upset:

'I saw the Staff, I know I did. And the conductor had it with him.' The conductor nodded unhappily. They were worried they might lose their jobs. The stationmaster opened his mouth to say something which was probably loud and cross, but just then there was a *PEEEP* from outside.

They all looked at each other and hurried out. Trams were not supposed to sound their whistles without their motormen being with them. What could have gone wrong now?

Pam's motorman hurried up to her: 'What's wrong, Pam?' He patted her, and checked her brake was on. 'What's happened?'

Pam looked at him and felt awful. He liked her best and she'd made him look so sad. Tina nudged her: 'Go on,' she hissed.

'It's my fault,' Pam said miserably. 'The Staff fell off me.'

'But why didn't you tell us?' asked her motorman. 'You know how important it is.' Pam couldn't look at him:

'I'm not green anymore. I liked being different. I don't like being red, it makes me look just like everyone else. And the Staff is red. Red's rubbish. I thought… I thought that if we didn't have a Staff I'd be a bit different again. I didn't want to get anyone into trouble. I didn't think it would cause all this fuss.

'And now you won't like me best any more,' she added. Trams didn't cry, but Pam thought she might try it.

'But, if the Staff had fallen off you, then Tina would have seen it,' said the stationmaster. 'Tina! Why didn't you say something?'

Tina looked hurt, but Pam said hurriedly: 'Tina did see it. She told me, but I told her not to tell. It's not her fault.' She looked at her motorman: 'I'm sorry. I didn't want to get

you and the conductor into trouble. Tina, I'm sorry.'

Her motorman patted her again: 'Oh Pam, you have been silly. But it was really brave to own up now. Tina, do you remember where the Staff fell off?'

'Yes,' said Tina proudly, 'it was near the waiting hut at Ballabeg.'

Just then the phone rang in the stationmaster's office.

The stationmaster hurried back to answer the phone, and found that it was Timothy Twenty. He was waiting nervously at the start of the Single Line Section, just as he'd been told to. Twain had passed him safely at Ballameanagh and whistled proudly. Timothy Twenty's motorman wanted to know what he should do now.

The stationmaster was relieved. He knew there couldn't be anything in the Single Line Section as no tram had left after Twain. He also knew where the Staff was. He told Timothy's motorman to go into the Single Line Section (slowly and carefully, just to be safe) and stop at Ballabeg to look for the Staff. Then he came back outside and talked to Pam's motorman and conductor:

'I've asked Timothy Twenty to look for the Staff. Meanwhile we have a service to run. Off you go to Ramsey.' He didn't look at Pam at all.

Pam felt very ashamed of herself as she headed out of Laxey. She had no passengers on board as they'd all been very cross about being so late and had decided not to go any further. Some of them had even (sshhh) transferred to the *Bus*. Pam was very ashamed. Trams and buses were very polite to each other but each wanted to get the most passengers. Having her passengers prefer to go by bus was very upsetting.

She felt Tina nudge her:

'Thank you, Pam.'

'What for?'

'For saying that I'd seen the Staff fall off you. And for not letting them be cross with me.'

'It was only fair: you did see it,' said Pam humbly. 'And thank you for not saying anything when I asked you not to.'

Just then a call came over the radio. It was Timothy Twenty's conductor. THEY'D FOUND THE STAFF!! It had been exactly where Tina had said it was. Now Timothy was in the Single Line Section With the Staff! Everything was alright now. Everything would be Safe.

Pam's conductor cheered, and shouted the good news to the Pam's motorman. He wasn't sure the motorman had heard it, but he made sure to tell him next time they stopped. Tina felt very proud that she'd been able to tell them where to look.

Pam was pleased that her motorman and conductor were not going to get into trouble for not having the Staff. But she was still very worried that they were cross with her.

Pam was very quiet as she hauled Tina along the line. There were people waiting at several of the stops and she stopped to let them get on, of course, but she didn't chat. Eventually her motorman said:

'What's the matter, Pam?'

'I'm wondering what's going to happen to me,' said Pam sadly. 'I've done a Bad Thing. They might lock me up in the back of Laxey shed.' The trams had all heard about the trams who had been left in Laxey shed for *years*. And sometimes Without Wheels. Pam didn't want that to happen to her.

'I don't think that will happen, Pam. Yes, you've been silly, but you tried to put it right. And you stood up for Tina. Besides, you're the only working Paddlebox we've got at the moment. And I still like you best.'

Pam thought about that. It was true. Anyone could be painted a different colour, but none of the other trams was a Paddlebox with steps like hers. She started to feel happier.

Then she remembered something else. The trams had been repainted lots of times. Working outside they got a bit wet and dirty and the weather wore their paint out, so they needed new coats every few years. Just like people really, she thought. Except that trams didn't grow bigger.

She thought about all the colours she might be in the future and cheered up. She might be green again before too long.

Besides, what she looked like didn't matter.

What was really important was that her motorman liked her.

She felt much happier.